Randy Lundy

Something for the Dark

Printed and bound in Canada.
The text of this book is printed on 100% post-consumer recycled paper with earth-friendly vegetable-based inks.

Cover art: "Conifer tree leaves" by dule964 / Adobe Stock

Cover design: Duncan Campbell, University of Regina Press

Interior design and layout:
John van der Woude, JVDW Designs

Series Editor: Randy Lundy
Copy Editor: Kelly Laycock

The text and titling faces are Arno, designed by Robert Slimbach.

Canadä

creative
SASKATCHEWAN

Library and Archives Canada Cataloguing in Publication

Title: Something for the dark / Randy Lundy.

Names: Lundy, Randy, 1967- author

Series: Oskana poetry & poetics.

Description: Series statement: Oskana poetry & poetics

Identifiers: Canadiana (print) 20250137410 | Canadiana (ebook) 20250137429 | ISBN 9781779400888 (softcover) | ISBN 9781779400901 (EPUB) | ISBN 9781779400918 (PDF)

Subjects: LCGFT: Poetry.

Classification: LCC PS8573.U54398 S66 2025 | DDC C811/.54—dc23

10 9 8 7 6 5 4 3 2 1

UNIVERSITY OF REGINA PRESS
University of Regina
Regina, Saskatchewan
Canada S4S 0A2
TELEPHONE: (306) 585-4758
FAX: (306) 585-4699
WEB: www.uofrpress.ca
EMAIL: uofrpress@uregina.ca

We acknowledge the support of the Canada Council for the Arts for our publishing program. We acknowledge the financial support of the Government of Canada. / Nous reconnaissons l'appui financier du gouvernement du Canada. This publication was made possible with support from Creative Saskatchewan's Book Publishing Production Grant Program.

How astonishing it is that language can almost mean,
and frightening that it does not quite.

from "The Forgotten Dialect of the Heart," Jack Gilbert

What do we do to those we need,

To those whose need of us endures
Even the knowledge of what we are?

. . . Out of whatever we have been
We will make something for the dark.

from "For Fran," Philip Levine

CONTENTS

Prelude

LETTER FROM KYOTO

for Nathan

A friend writes from Japan. A poem from Fushimi Inari-taisha.

You want to tell him you first read *Fushimi* as *Fukushima*. But that was a mistake. He writes of the red gates and stone foxes with the keys to prosperity and worldly wealth in their mouths. Not cesium-infused tuna sushi, or the thyroid cancer risks for infants exposed to iodine isotopes. The wall around the reactor site was thirty-three feet high. The largest wave to make landfall peaked at forty-three. Arrived fifty minutes after the quake.

Meanwhile here in Saskatchewan, the place both of you call home, *Land of the Living Skies* is just a caption for the tourist brochures and licence plates. No one's thought through what the *Living* in the motto really means. Is it an assertion of the eternal fusion of space-time into a four-dimensional continuum? Is the sky that which moves without being moved? Aristotle's prime mover that preceded Descartes's clockwork universe?

No matter, here human beings are no better, no worse than they have ever been.

Take the Gunnar mine site, the uranium open-pit Sheol on the north shore of Lake Athabasca, shuttered in 1964, as if it was a window we could close because we couldn't bear staring through it for eternity. The mine shut down after nearly a decade of producing yellowcake to fuel the American side of the arms race. Yellowcake to produce heat for the Cold War that delimited the horizons of our childhoods. Superpowers defined the climate of our lives, the way climate change does for children today.

That mine abandoned, padlocked behind a chain-link fence—full of holes like every alibi—as if the world could be kept in or out. As if any of us can walk away without carrying the taint of what has been deemed no longer of value or use. For fifty years, no one thought to clean up the four million–plus tonnes of tailings—adrift in wind and suspended in water for the entire five decades you've been alive.

You wonder about the half-life, the decay rate of human ingenuity.

Today is one of those days for you. They come and go like sparrows in the cedars. Coffee and a cigarette. And, as always, the dogs, who raise their noses to catch the multitude of scents carried in the river of air that flows from Alberta's foothills to Manitoba's escarpments, right through this village on the south-Saskatchewan plains. You are thinking of friends and family far away. Some as far away as death—just another someplace-else for which you can't find the mailing address.

A thunderstorm rolls in from the west at six a.m. The sky grows light before growing dark again. Time to take yourself away, into retreat.

Everything frays at the seams. Landscapes, memories, desires fuse and separate. Like smoke, consciousness floats and mingles with dream. Is this what vision means? Like Job, you want to rend your clothing and weep. To bathe your head in dirt—the glacial-deposit, hill-top soil. Prickly pear cacti stand around aimlessly with hands raised in praise of something you can neither see nor name. You sit in silence for days on the ash pile of the fire that kept you warm through the night's cold hours. The light now gone into a darkness dense as the iron-nickel core in the heart of a misanthrope. A hate that creeps each day, old and persistent as lichen on a stone's face.

You are barren-mouthed and empty-eyed. Your spirit call, a song, is answered not by silence but by the voice of a nighthawk in the near distance, with the still-living body of a moth halfway down its throat. Your mind speckled like the feathers of that bird. Mind camouflaged from itself. Down below, Buffalo Pound Lake laps at the clay shoreline and the rock weir that crosses the marsh at the south end. Red-winged blackbirds cling to the drift and sway of reeds. Up in the coulee, a few bison lie in a patch of aspen and willow, drowsing in the fenced enclosure. paskwâwi-mostos. Tokens of entry into a past that brokers no admittance, a history that still dwells everywhere, grazes in the evening on sun-bleached grass that grows from the dusty marrow of our ancestors.

You want to tell your friend that sometimes distances collapse like buildings before the onslaught of an enormous ocean wave, a kind of rage caused by the slip-slide of tectonic plates. Except what you feel is not rage but something else with just as much ferocity. You can see him as he stands before the first gate, at the foot of what is called a mountain but is only a low hill. He pays his fee, enters, and begins to climb. You feel in your own feet his body's weight, feel the bend of his knees as he walks, passes through each of the ten thousand torii gates. You feel the pace and rate of his breathing when the path becomes steep—in through the nose and out through the mouth.

You want to tell him the *Spirit of Permeability* is the only god. And without jealousy. The walls of our flesh, our hearts, each of our cells—all walls are really just gates. Maybe it's no answer, but Buddha and Bashō, Rilke and Blake, each say the same thing—for better and for worse, there is no threshold between the sacred and profane.

*paskwâwi-mostos—bison

HUNGER

It is the first sure sign of spring, the woman thinks.
The first robin she has spotted. But it's lying on the
sidewalk beside her house, taken by a peregrine in
the early morning before she woke from another
night of bad dreams. The raptor must have been
disturbed at its kill, since it left the carcass headless
with only a portion of the breast devoured. An omen
of this new season of her life, she is certain.

And you are sitting on your deck admiring the dog's
ears that hang like a pair of temple bells. Her body
is the only place of worship that you could stand
to set foot in. Mastiff cross, molosser-type dog
bred for war, for blood and flesh. Yet you live
with her in peace. There is no ownership here,
though she sleeps by your side at night and sits
right now near your feet on the back deck, where
you smoke cigarettes and drink your coffee, black.

So, what's this poem about anyway? You have a right
to ask, dear friend. Is the poem about the woman
and the dead bird she has found? Is it about the man
who sits quietly with a dog watching the clouds pass?

Winter has left in everything a deep hunger. Once
again, spring has come and gone and summer, as always,
requires eating—every single being making a meal
of the kinds of things the kind of thing it is demands.

A KIND OF KNOWING

In the long hours and days of prairie winter you
find the darkness you have craved.

You find joy in the bodies of crows punctuating the air.

Just last week, driving the grid road, you spotted five of them
congregated around the body of a road-killed deer in the ditch,
the largest bird perched at the tip of the tallest rib, a strip of meat
in its beak, a red prayer flag hanging limp in the February wind.

Let's get this straight, you are not ungrateful. You love the
world and want it to be just what and as it is. You want the
deer to live its life, then die unwilling and unknowing in a
sudden flurry of violence. You want the crows to feast.

Whatever you are is not broken in the ditch, unseeing, eyes
mirror-blank except for the endless depth and breadth of sky
reflected there. But you live in close proximity to that.

You are the winter-brittle tongues of grass, unspeaking, pressed
beneath the weight of the deer's body, its particular kind of knowing.

DIAGNOSIS

We are the fat, laughing Buddha—Budai—each of us,
the one we all recognise. But without the wisdom
or compassion.

kayâs, our minds closed like
the eye of a gull, dying
on the lakeshore, red-and-
white-striped fishing hook in
its throat, trailing a fibre optic
filament of line like a silent,
transparent tongue from
its mouth.

(Pause here to breathe.)

We have forgotten, don't
even realise, we need to
open our ahcahk, yes, like
an awakening eye, or like
a hand becoming not-fist—

a palm opening to blue sky
and the blaze of pine-pollen
yellow, pulsing drum of sun.

*kayâs—a long time ago
*ahcahk—spirit

LOOKING

The not-yet-stirring-to-life-this-spring
branches of an unidentified bush
outside the window, above the desk
where you sit.

Look.

Books will do you no good
nor the memory of books
—Hanshan and Du Fu—
not in this time and place,

the only time and place you know,
the ones in which this world
is a house that's never become
a home for us

and is on fire.

LABOUR DAY

Low, grey, heavy cloud and rain
to begin September. Stiff, unrelenting
wind out of the southeast.

All but the last half-dozen or so
plums fallen from the tree, split open
on the unstained wooden deck
where patches of pale green moss
have thinly taken hold, the planks
that support your weight slick
and a danger to the bones.

Conscious of the threat of a slip and a fall,
you shuffle your feet like an old man trying
to get to wherever it is he is trying to go.

You'd like for the broken fruit to be
a metaphor for something, but it's not,
unpicked for the first time in a decade,
overripe and food for the flies that gather
and buzz. Your neglect, the nectar
that sustains their desire
to survive.

This morning, it took all your strength
to get out of bed. Hungover from
another day of sobriety.

But you had work to do:
the dogs needed to be fed,
a pack of cigarettes to be smoked,
a pot of coffee to be heated on the stove.

And your teacher is dead; you must grieve.

Today has drained you of enthusiasm for words
that aspire to be more than what they indicate,
or gesture toward, at least.

Even if you could manage to make them
representational, it would be enough.
This word equals that thing—a simple formula
would be enough. But you feel meaning shift
and decentre itself, like the weather,
independent of your mind.

Blackbirds are flocking at the edges of the fields
that surround the village you soon will leave,
the small, quiet, darkened house that has been,
like the painted turtle's shell,
your only home in this life.

Flee is too dramatic a word
for what the birds will do. They will migrate
from the northern prairie to the southern
States and Mexico—Texas and Chiapas.

While here, in Saskatchewan, winter will descend,
once again, as it's always done,
and will seem endless.

Make a list to prepare yourself:

1. There will be dark and cold; it will go on for days and months.
2. There will be death; it will stand for nothing other than itself.
3. The raven perched on the power pole considers its next move; it does not know your name.
4. Time is not a mind or map, does not remember itself, what it's left behind, or where it's been.

AN OLD MAN'S THEORY OF LANGUAGE

A red-breasted nuthatch tapping
on the weathered wooden fence,

a ruby-throated hummingbird hovering
above the open-throated lilies,

a downy woodpecker climbing
the trunk of the birch tree.

The birds come and go like thoughts, but they are not thoughts.
They are not words. Bodies come first, then words
follow them into the world.

Delicate-boned, feathered bodies—
the *always already there*. Here.

On the wings of itinerant birds, syllables
rise into the skies of our minds, come
to rest in our mouths, nest
on our tongues.

Plum tree and ponderosa pine, branch tips and elongated
needles brittle in the minus-thirty-degree February cold
of the prairie. Standing outside with a cigarette and cup
of coffee, your fingers quickly grow numb, but nothing
approaching the dumb, mute meditation of roots in their
stalled, frozen reach toward an understanding of eternity,
an almost-union that you are tempted to call *divine*.

And you are thinking of the woman sixty-five miles away,
sitting in her parents' kitchen, fire burning in the woodstove, a
mixed-breed shepherd dog lying near her feet as she works
on the *New York Times* Sunday-morning crossword, yellow-
shafted pencil held between forefinger and thumb.

She is stalled by seven across—an eight-letter word for
never-ending. It should be easy. The solution is *eternity*.
It should be simple. Eternity.

When the answer for seven across arrives, it comes to her like
a revelation, something she always knew but could not quite
articulate. With care, she prints each letter in the appropriate box
on the page. She reaches for the teapot and refills her cup, sighs
with something like relief, as if the world, a temporarily foreign
and unrecognisable place, has returned to its ordered state.

The dog stirs. The woman looks at the word she has just
made appear on the page—*eternity*—and wonders if humans
shouldn't be more concerned with the preoccupations of the
dog's world—a bowl filled with food, someone's foot resting
on her back, and, later in the day, a walk in the almost blinding
light of the mid-morning sun ablaze on the hard-crusted snow.

What you and the woman know is that the human world exists somewhere between stilled deep roots and whatever lies beyond the cosmic microwave radiation. Whatever that is, it is not god and does not wear a human face.

You want to tell the woman about the single chickadee who arrived in the branches of the maple tree just after dawn this morning. One unremarkable bird that survived the night and then called with its winter-thin voice even though there seemed to be no one but you to hear.

WHEN YOU OWN NOTHING BUT HUNGER

You are out with a coffee and cigarette when a great horned owl swoops into the spruce in the neighbours' backyard. They are away this afternoon and you are alone, so you walk up to the fence and gaze over it into the frost-encrusted branches, brittle but still green in the end-of-November prairie cold.

The owl has flushed three pigeons from the tree, and in a panicked riffle shuffle of wings, they disappear into the snow falling thick and slow as thinking in the grey light. When the predator again takes flight, it clutches nothing but emptiness in its talons, the slow burn of a coal-seam fire in its gut.

WHAT FALLING REVEALS

This morning the leaves drop straight down.
No wind. The sound on the roof
like the padding of feral feet.

Autumn. Middle of the Canadian prairie.
Nothing novel in any of that. No news,
once again, from here. Nothing to see.
No car wreck. No bombs. No shuddering
of the earth pulling buildings down
around the heads of huddled children.

Do you envy the suffering of others?
Your own local disasters are quieter.

You have left one house empty
to move into the emptiness of another,
your life boxed and crated, carted
across a city asleep.

You read somewhere: *Grief is the door to wisdom.*
You have no key for that lock but have been admitted,
anyway, into a country in which you recognise nothing
and have no rights.

Pre-dawn light. On branches draped
over the fence on the east side of the yard
the faces of shrivelled apples. A broken, long-
abandoned wasps' nest hanging like the body
of a headless owl.

AFTER READING SUSAN GLICKMAN'S "THE DAYTIME MOON"

The first thing is this: the moon
is neither modest nor tenacious,
does not long for anyone, least of all
you. Still, there it is, mid-afternoon,
powdered, pale-faced, the cause of
tides and nothing else—not madness.
It is no floating womb, but reflects sunlight
while tethered by nothing resembling love
to this small blue planet on which we turn.

After your walk, on the news, Notre-Dame burns.
We look on, we watch. *How sad,* we think. *How sad.*
And "the forest," the roof frame, constructed of 1,300 oaks—
each three hundred to four hundred years old when cut for the
greater glory
of god—burns and turn to ash, and it's not for the trees
we grieve. Ancient certainly, but what is a few hundred years
when measured against eternity? Nothing. Less than ash.

We eat our dinners in front of our screens, and meanwhile,
around the planet wildfires burn and species blink, flicker,
die out like stars we've never seen.

ARS POETICA

Almost-full-now moon,
intestine of jet trail dragging
from its side, twisting
behind.

Like a gut-shot animal.
Like a childhood.

A father stricken
with anxiety and depression.

Three hundred pounds of suffering
locked behind the door of a single-
wide trailer. With his boy.

And no brother, no sister, no mother
to turn to.

Enough pain to fill a room.
Two hearts. The term *broken*
comes to mind, but that's just
melodrama, and you know it,
the theme of every country tune
that kept you company
through your youth,
all those "Wasted Days
and Wasted Nights."

And John Hooker's
"Whiskey and Wimmen"
over and over again

got you exactly
where you were trying
to go.

Years of booze and confusion
and no woman foolish enough
to sit with you through
that madness.

In the end, what's true is
you loved the man, even more
fiercely once he died.

His own heart a gas-filled mine
shaft, exploded by the pressure
of all the things he could not say:

I'm lonely. Help me.

Just simple words like that
might have been enough.

Sometimes a single spark is all it takes
to set off the blaze that consumes us.
An explosion of gas and dust that leaves
nothing but the scent of death and flame.

What's true is
your father's to blame
for none of it,
what you made
of yourself.

So tonight, you stand on the back deck,
looking up at the sky. The moon
a wounded animal in your mind's eye.

And you know
you have to speak
a different dialect
of this language
that's tried
to destroy you.

HOW YOUR DAY WAS

Cricket chirp, a kind of squeak or creak,
in the far darkness this evening,

like the music of the spheres that time
god was absent and forgot to oil the gears

of the cosmic-sized machine that keeps
the whole damned thing turning,

even without a hand on the crank
and no one at the wheel.

SPECIES PROBLEM, THE AUDIENCE THAT WASN'T

I went into the lodge, into the cave, climbed to the high peak of the holy mountaintop, and came out, came down, without a dream, without a vision of which I could speak. Saint of the Everyday, Shaman of the Quotidian, no one wanted to hear that every god that had ever been was in the rock and the root, the seed and the tree, that each god arrives on the black-padded feet of a dog. No one wanted to hear of the divinity of a clay mug that any one of us can hold in our hands and feel the warmth of eternity seep through the glaze, that the blaze of sun on the steel side of a grain bin at the edge of a field of yellow-blooming canola or the thick scent of clover is a transfiguration of the world.

It's a species problem. There are no ears to hear, no eyes to see.

What is it you want, dear reader, my friend?
I come to you robed in an animal's skin, with
antlers tied to my head. I shake the rattle, beat
the drum, and sing. Still, the only words I have
for you are these, the simplest ones, in the same
language you speak.

Look. Nothing is hidden here.

A Tennessee warbler
flits among the branches
and leaves of the plum,
with its just now ripening
fruit, gobbling insects
to fuel its journey
from Saskatchewan
to the tidewaters
of the Gulf Coast.

Your whole body is a lung, skin breathing in
the moisture of last night's rain.
Nothing remains
to say.

ON FORGIVENESS

for Patrick

The orange flame of the female cardinal's beak.
You cannot speak of the places you have been.
The things you have seen and done. You will not.

Your own heart was the last of all the stops. Here.
How could that be? Left only, now, with questions.
And there, in those dark chambers, you found no

forgiveness. That rare thing your hands never held.
These hands that reveal themselves as nothing. But.
The bird wings its ashen body into the green cedar.

A GUIDE TO SELF-CARE

The three dogs plow their noses in the fourteen
inches of still-soft snow that fell overnight,
searching for wind-fallen apples no larger
than cherries. When they begin to lift their
feet from the cold, bring them with you into
the warmth of the small, stuccoed house.
Invite them in.

The animals have not chosen to live
here, in the silences that fill your home.
You have chosen. However, you did not
choose, either, to live with this self you have
more than fifty years now, the two of you
eating and sleeping together and not always
comfortably. A strange kind of marriage.

The dogs have tried to teach you. Just now,
one of them has come and laid her head in your lap.
When you scratch her ears, she nuzzles your hand
with her black nose and licks your flat palm.

Remember this moment. Do not make again
that same assumption you have so many times.
Do not mistake affection for submission.
Not with the dogs. Not with yourself.

AUTUMN AWAKENING

Mid-September morning,
northern prairie, southern
Saskatchewan, damp and cold.
You sit outside with a coffee
and a smoke, wearing a felt-
lined denim jacket as three
crows drift by, black in a way
only crows can be, against blue
sky, sun glinting off wings.

In the distance, combines sit
idle at the edges of fields,
sinking into soft soil, deep
into thought, the crops
cut and in the bins, each
a corrugated steel hive
filled with seed, still alive
but just barely, communities
of grain with eons of memory,
their own histories of the land.

Something in the air
changed overnight.

All the temples that had been everywhere
are in rapid retreat,

and, right now, you know what it means to feel
like an empty shell, a husk, like a man
at the end of what turned out to be
only a brief seasonal warmth.

Today, you are a bronze
bell without a tongue—
defined by an absence.

You will never be rung.

I DON'T EVEN THINK OF YOU THAT OFTEN

I do not know where you are,
and I really do not care. I just
wanted to write to tell you
this. It's not that I don't hope
that you got everything you
wanted, everything you deserved.
And you wanted much, and you
deserved much, too, so filled
with life that I could not touch.

Once, you asked me why
the sky was blue. I asked you
what it meant that the sky
was blue. It was just the first
of many misunderstandings.
They grew prolific as the blades
of grass the wind passes over
and through, until they are no
more. Just like us. Me and you.

Once, you told me something
I've never forgotten, that you loved
your brand of Christianity, your
Catholicism, because it meant
you could be anywhere in the world
and walk into a church and feel at home.
It's one of the reasons I could no
longer continue to walk with you.
It doesn't mean there was no love.

Still, I could never understand why
one would want to travel across
the globe, across the many
latitudes and longitudes, only
to feel at home, to avoid the
inevitable loneliness that comes
from leaving everything familiar
behind. I've never understood
wanting god always at your side.

So, I am writing this to you
across the great and the small distances
that separate us, and always have.
I want you to know, after all these years,
I live alone, with only a couple of dogs
for companionship. Dogs and the moon.
Cigarettes, which you could never accept,
and coffee. A meal of bread and cheese.
But no wine. My work goes well. I am alive.

I don't even think of you
that often.

THINKING OF THE BOTTICELLI GIRL, TEN YEARS LATER

Waxing final third. The moon. Your life, too, my friend. In
the first fifty-one years, you got so little right. All the friends,
lovers, family members who didn't die, you alienated. If it
wasn't ego, simple unabashed pride, it was alcohol, whisky-
and beer-fuelled nights, the falling down and the fights,
sometimes with fists, but mostly with words. And maybe ego
and out-of-control drunk come down to the same thing.

A decade ago, in Florence, in the Uffizi, wandering the Botticelli
rooms, ten to fourteen, eventually settling in front of the *Birth of
Venus,* holding the hand of a woman half your age, her first time
away from home. What were you thinking? On an Italian tour,
with a teenager, and you forty years old? Did you believe she was
born of the sea, blown by the winds, her body a perfect pearl?

If nothing else, her body was precious as a pearl and as white, and
among your many regrets, the nakedness on the overnight train to
Naples isn't one of them. Still, what is it you hoped to gain from
the whole affair? Was it just sex, a thrill ride on the roller coaster
of some mid-life crisis? You didn't feel you were in mid-life, or in
crisis, and perhaps that was the whole problem, not knowing the
ground upon which you stood. You didn't really feel or know much
of anything, except the ache in your bones when the booze wore off.

Tonight, last week of December, you stand alone in the
yard, except for the company of two dogs. Looking up at the
moon. The bare-branched ash and maples standing silently
by. No wind tonight, for a change. Hands stuffed into your
pockets and a cigarette hanging from your lip. And what are
the myths in which you now believe? Not a woman's body.
Not the wisdom of the Greeks. This is it. This is all you believe.
The trees. A couple of dogs. Cup of coffee. A cigarette.

All you know is this: it's three nights past solstice, the light is growing imperceptibly longer each day, and what's left of the moon is rising in the sky. Beneath your feet, even through the frozen ground, you can feel the approach of a freight train. In the distance, a lone coyote howl. The train passes by and into the deep night. The fields are still and quiet, again.

It was a liquor-fuelled, pool-shooting, cowboy-boots-hitting-the-floor-before-the-clothes-came-off kind of weekend. Beer and whisky. Bohemian and Jack Daniel's, straight. Downtown hotel bar, where the down-and-outers and the Indians liked to hang out. Later, staggering back to your third-floor apartment, with two bottles of cheap red wine, the music a mix of Leonard Cohen singing "Hallelujah" and Patsy Cline singing "Crazy," along with Waylon Jennings (your choice) and 16 Horsepower (hers). You've had too many nights like this, though not all of them landed you in bed with a young Jewish woman, daughter to a visiting professor. Too many nights like this one, and most of the names of the leading ladies have been forgotten. But not this one. You won't say her name here because you've already said too much. Enough to violate her dignity and leave you feeling ashamed and vulnerable, a slight tremble in your hands.

What can you say, since you won't say her name? Her hair was down to her waist and dark, curled like the eddies in a river you remember from your youth; chestnut eyes aflame in the candlelight; skin white as milk spilled and glistening in moonlight. It all sounds too good to be true, but that's how you remember it. And those are the details you remember. Not the words she spoke but the heavy, wet scent that hung in the air after sex.

So, what are you trying to say here, that it was love, found and lost in a matter of three days?

If you knew where she was, how to reach her, you'd like to tell her these things: you are sitting in your modest house, in a town of five hundred, alone except for the dogs, listening to Hank III singing "Ridin' the Wave," and the fiddle screech and the mad-frantic banjo picking, as if the instrument is on speed or meth, reminds you of the music of that band from Denver to which she introduced you. It was the music that made you think of her.

You'd like to tell her that as you write this, you hope someday she reads it and recognises herself and knows you remember her. You'd like to tell her the young man you were back then wasn't even a man but still a small, frightened boy and that you are not him anymore. That you wouldn't want to be, except for that weekend with her.

LOCKDOWN NOTE—TO A FORMER LOVER, ANGLICAN OR CATHOLIC

Down on my hands and knees
as if praying but really cleaning
the toilet for the first time in weeks,
the white porcelain cold beneath
the rag I keep for just this purpose,
the inner bowl streaked with brown,
the colour of wet askiy, mud and peat,
and on the underside of the seat,
now raised like a hand in praise,
golden speckles like dried sunlight.

This is why you could never love me.

Now, I remember cleanliness is next
to godliness. I apologise for this desecration.
For the last month, I have been writing a poem.

*askiy—earth

AT THE POETRY READING

Someone asks you about *the gifts of silence and looking.*

Truth is they were imposed, gifted to you by a father who
spent hours, day after day, sitting at a kitchen table in a
fourteen-foot-wide trailer, one hand holding a cup of coffee
in front of him and a cigarette hanging forgotten in the other,
staring out the single-pane window and seeing nothing but
his past, a long path to the loneliness that engulfed him.

Your only choice: to imitate, to be silent
and watchful. Wait for an escape.

But he's dead now, gone more than a quarter century, his
body turned to clay, a trickle of chemicals leeched into the
aquifer below the graveyard, a clearing carved like a scar into
the poplar and aspen. And memory has been its own kind of
danger for you. Neural pathways cut like game trails on a hillside.
Depression a constellation in the night sky of your mind.

What calls you back is always outside.

Right now, it is the thought of yesterday's walk with the
dogs and the drive back home. Four pronghorns on the
grid road as you drove north in the heat, a haze of dust and
the last of the moisture sucked out of the land after three
months of drought. Their narrow faces yellow-tan and
brown like the dried grasses along the stagnant creek in the
shallow valley you just left, the wild oats and the sage.

Their white rumps as they walk away are muscled stories,
their bodies postcards from this world and the next. The
writing on those cards is illegible, but the audience
hopes it's some version of *Wish you were here.*

LISTENING TO THE HIGH NOON SINGERS

for Damon

The little hound, a treeing Tennessee brindle, Grace, short for Graciela, named after Graciela Iturbide, the Mexican photographer of indigeneity, Bravo's student, who turned to the art after the death of her six-year-old daughter, Claudia. Isn't that often how it works, my friend? Grief transforms the person into the artist. Into *Our Lady of the Iguanas*. That's how the ritual works. Not some conscious choice we make.

You pour your tea, light a candle, burn some sage, and put on music—the High Noon Singers from Thunderchild Reserve. Yes, that Thunderchild, piyesiw awasis, defender of the Cree, the nêhiyawak. That one who tore down the church on his people's land. The singers are pounding out an intertribal, and Grace raises her voice in a guttural howl, accompanying the men's high pitch. Your girl sings along right until the end of the song, the last note, and you want to hear more.

So, you go to the computer, to YouTube.com, and there they are, the same singers, at the Sioux Valley Powwow in 2012. Seven young men and one much older, who you guess must be a father or an uncle to some of the younger ones gathered in that tight circle. The men's mud-brown skins. And the old one, you want to know his story. You want to know his name. You never will. You hear only the voices. You hear only the song. And it is not your song. No one has gifted it to you. You have no rights here.

*piyesiw awasis—Thunderchild
*nêhiyawak—Cree people

The Sioux Valley Powwow. 2012. You were not there. You can't remember what you were doing that weekend, likely sitting in a bar in the city. Drunk. Again. You can't remember the name of the place. Or the name of the woman. The colour of her eyes. Barely remember the two of you waking up in the same bed. She must have had a child, must have made you a cup of coffee in the barely-there, pre-dawn light. Before you left.

All the hours and years spent that way. Another Indian man, lost. Another generation. All that suffering. All that pain. Be thankful *that* day is not *this* day. Be grateful and pray. Do it in this way.

AN ACT OF GRACE

Like a wood lily, you are shy, even when
open-throated and singing. But that's a lie,
a fallacy, since lilies are never shy, just quiet
in the way flowers are, and are, thus, not like us.
Lying is an old habit left over from childhood
when you didn't want to admit to your father
that you had stolen the pack of gum from your
aunt and uncle's store, which was also a gas
station, named Starlite, just south of that
boreal town whose noisy machines lived
on constant meals provided by the forest.
That's how the people lived, too. Trees
as fuel for a hunger that would not die.
If you thought that the cosmic stupidity
of childhood, the lying and the greed,
would end, you've had fifty years now
to learn otherwise. The mistakes continue
to pile up, to accrete. Adulthood, for our
species, never seems to arrive. The question
of whether or not the ignorance is forgiven
is not one you can answer, and what would
it mean, in any case, for you to forgive your
self: for all the betrayals, of others, yes, but
betrayals that were ultimately enacted
against everything in you that might have
been best? These lines are getting the
discussion nowhere. Let's put it like this:
wood lilies are not shy. You, too, have not
been shy about your own failings as the kind
of creature you are. You shall not forgive
yourself. And there's no one else to do it.

Rain late last evening, near the end of April, and a light freeze overnight. This morning the windows feathered with frost as if the world had left fingerprints detailing its dreams of flight, and out for a cigarette with your first coffee, two dogs, and evaporate rising in the backyard like smoke from a bush fire up in the Pasqua hills, among the trees, just north and east of the peat bog where your cousin Elmer works, and where he sets up trail cams to catch ghost-like images of the caribou whose tracks he's seen, where they come to calve in spring, the tangled undergrowth and the soft, wet land protection from the local wolf pack. And you are reading an article about two young female poets—one from Greenland and one from the Marshall Islands—lives destroyed by the melting ice and others by the steadily rising tides. Communities thousands of miles apart. But violence is like that—it works up close and at great distances like spookily conjoined subatomic particles. For some reason, you think of a colleague at work, her saying, *I love Indigenous cultures. They're so beautiful,* and you want to tell her to just keep it to herself, that you don't give a fuck, that the people don't need the wihtikow hunger of her appreciation and praise. *Save it for your god,* you want to say. You witnessed what she did with the old woman's teachings about sage: she and her small, like-minded gang ran to the nearest bush, threw down some tobacco, and stripped it bare, then sat in the shade of a pickup truck and gossiped—they huddled and clucked—while plucking the leaves from thin branches. And you realise this image is an insult to chickens everywhere, but at least you've still got your sense of humour, even though you are feeling bitter this morning, like the taste on your fingers after lighting a smudge, and you do nothing but sit down to fiddle around with words, while the controlled spin of the world whisks all of us into a future devoid of human care and concern.

*wihtikow—a cannibal spirit

A NOTE ON THE USE OF THE TERM *GENOCIDE*

A few scattered flakes of snow
and you want to say they drift down
like ash from the chimneys of Auschwitz
or Birkenau, but you cannot claim that
history. Perhaps you have no right even
to write a poem in the long shadow of that
time.

And what of the sixty million dead in the Americas
in the first hundred years after contact? But that's
too abstract. Just statistics.

You'll be accused of confusing, of conflating.
Let it be so.

What about the hands
of each and every woman who had her child torn
away from her by disease, hunger, or by another's hands?
(It still goes on today.)

Can you write about that? What about those trembling
hands? A trembling like nothing you can say, not in this
or any other language, no words for that kind of pain.

Let's do the math: that's six hundred thousand dead each
year; fifty thousand dead per month; twelve thousand dead
per week, almost two thousand dead each day.

Perhaps it is impossible to write a poem about such things.
Certainly, if you try, you should not speak of trees and birds
or dogs, or the violence of your childhood home. Your Irish-
Norwegian father. Your nêhiyaw mother. And fifty years later,
you, still just a frightened, confused three-year-old boy. Do not
speak of it. Do not try to make a link. Connect nothing.

Fortunately, most of those who might read this will not recognise it
as a poem.
Still, if you managed to read this far, if you remember one thing
when you reach
the end of this page, I ask that it be this: the pain we each carry,
brother or sister,
the pain in every brown face, is not just our own.

And this is no confessional poem.

AN ANSWER TO THE MASTER, WHILE WONDERING WHERE ALL THE INDIANS WENT

for Charles Wright

It's our job to try to corral mystery, your Master says. And who are you to say he's wrong, acolyte? But you know he's wrong, even if you haven't got the courage to say so. Of course, he grew up in Tennessee and Virginia, on the *King James* and Cranmer's *Common Book of Prayer*. So, you suppose that must have something to do with it, what with us all being hung up on our childhoods as we are, and he admits he's been *corralled* by that language ever since.

But you grew up in the bush, on the banks of the rivers, all three of them. Not the Tigris, the Euphrates, and the Shatt al-Arab, but the Fir, the Etomami, and the Red Deer. The posts and rails of the Master's corral reach back to the cradle of civilisation. Your own path is no more deep or wide than the Red Deer in spring, just when the ice breaks with a roar, which you might compare to the voice of the lion of a god. But you know it's just the ice letting go, in the middle of the night, when you are ten years old.

The wolves are back in droves in the Porcupine Hills, numerous like they might have been a hundred years ago. But there's no one left to tell those stories, and Hudson Bay, Saskatchewan, is not the kind of place about which anyone ever bothers to write anything down. There was the fur trading post near Erwood, open for business in 1757, the North West Company's at the mouth of the Etomami, in 1790, and maybe a South Company post on the opposite bank. That's when civilisation arrived.

But it never stayed. Hell, by the time you and your father moved there in 1974, even in your unschooled childhood perceptions, the place sure didn't seem civilised exactly. You and your dad lived in a room on the third floor of the Red Deer Hotel because there wasn't a house unoccupied. Trees to be cut and lumber prices high, three mills running 24/7, and young, single men coming from far and wide, from right across the country, because there was money to be made. Whisky-fuelled fights in the streets.

But you've lost your place. What you meant to say is something you'll never have the chance to say to Mr. Wright's face. That he's wrong. That mystery is not something to be corralled. That it's not a matter of wrangling. That's a gunslinger's myth. You want to tell the Master: our job is to stand at a distance, avert our gaze, and wait. If mystery desires, it'll come up close behind you like those wild horses near Fort Walsh in the Cypress Hills once did. If mystery is interested, if it wants to, it will sidle up right behind you, nuzzle the back of your neck with its wide dark nostrils, and give you a sniff.

BACH AND MY FATHER

after Paul Zimmer

I don't like to think of my father
in the dark down by the river, alone
except for the black border collie
flattened on the ground, pinned
between his knees, her breathing.
And the gleaming ball-peen hammer
with its worn hickory wood handle
gripped in his fist, poised in the air
above his right ear, silhouetted
against the full moon
no one is there to see.

Three days later, she returned mid-
afternoon, a bit of fur missing from
the centre of her somehow-unbroken
skull, a small bald patch about the size
of my father's thick, callused fingertip.

She was meant to die, and I didn't
even want her was what he told me.
If I wanted to keep her, wanted her
not to *go away*, I'd better show more
that I cared. We never did that
for each other, showed that we cared,
my father and me. Never kissed or
hugged, didn't even shake hands.
Something unspoken but threatening
in the press of one man's flesh against
another's.

What I like to remember is the time
he walked through my front door
years later. I am an adult, listening
to music—partitas for solo violin—
and writing poems like I sometimes
do. Except this never happened.
He died early and alone at the back
of the trailer I grew up in.

"The Old Rugged Cross" played at the funeral.
He never heard a single note of Bach. Never said,
How beautiful, while gazing out the window
at rain and sparrows huddled
in the branches of a pine.

WHAT LUNDY WOULD BE

after Paul Zimmer

When asked as a child what I wanted to be,
I did not answer a doctor, a priest, a magician.
I wanted to be Jesus Christ himself and would
say so: *I want to be the Son of God!* I wanted
to be a healer, a layer of hands upon the wounded,
those delimbed like a tree, disembowelled like
a gut-shot squirrel, to raise the dead scattered
along the bush paths and vacant lots of small-
town Saskatchewan, where we fought the Battle
of the Little Bighorn or Wounded Knee, re-enacting
those scenes we saw on TV, late-night black and white,
while our parents drank on the back porch.

And more than once, I laid hands upon General
George Armstrong Custer and proclaimed, *Rise!*
Rise and go forth, and bring your light into the
darkness! Thank you, Gideons, for sending your
evangelical angels to our small school, in our small
logging town, in our far-away-from-it-all outpost
nestled in the edge of the mixed-boreal forest,
where, with bloodied nose, scraped knuckles,
and torn jeans, I wrestled the schoolyard bully
on the mud-puddled playground. Thank you
for your mythology of everlasting life rescued
from the fists of Eugene and the cross on Calvary.

When asked as a child what I wanted to be,
I never answered, *What I am. An Indian.*

These days, no one asks me the question.
These days, I wrestle no angels. I wrestle

with words. And no one is saved.

MY GRANDFATHER AS MYTH

after Paul Zimmer's "Planets"

As a child, I never stepped out with my grandfather
from the front door of his house, the house that
travelled Saskatchewan, from homestead to town
and, finally, to another, larger town, to be nearer
the children and grandchildren. The house moved
like a constellation, followed like a loyal dog, until
the key, like a leash, was passed into the hands
of strangers.

I never stood with him to look at the stars
in the autumn sky, Orion wheeling in the dark
above the rows of potato plants, their elephant
ears veined and flapping in a breeze.

I never stood with him on a summer afternoon
to count the logging trucks passing on the highway,
hauling wood from the hills—white spruce and jack pine—
to one of three mills running full-time in the '70s.

James or Jim—none of us grandkids
dared call him either, his name like a rumour,
whispered only to one another, out of earshot
of any adult, a name like a myth, his blue eyes
pale and cold as glacier ice.

I never stepped out with my grandfather, clinging
to his farmer's finger thick as a root in my fist.

I accept you died before I could know you, before I grew into a man.
I accept that had you lived longer I would never have known you.
I accept I carry forward only your silence as inheritance.

We must have had a conversation,
one, at least, though I cannot recall.

And now, I think it must have been you who taught me
to make of silence something rather than nothing,
something *from* nothing,

the way all of it—the stars, the planets, everything living—
    came to be.

AS A CHILD I NEVER HAD FRUIT FOR BREAKFAST EXCEPT WHEN WE ATE OUT WHICH WAS RARE UNLESS WE WERE TRAVELLING AND THEN SOMETIMES THERE WAS A SLICE OF SOMETHING ON THE EDGE OF THE RESTAURANT PLATE

Moon, thin slice of orange,
nearly transparent. You can almost,
but not quite, see galaxies behind it.

Birch tree trunk somehow darker than
the surrounding night. A final cicada
creaks—once, twice, then silence—

and your father, stubbornly,
still dead.

Leaving Billings, Montana, you take the exit onto the I-90 East,
rather than staying on the I-94 toward Bismarck, North Dakota.
It's not the first time in life you've taken the proverbial wrong turn.
And when you reach the Crow Agency, just past Hardin, you realise
your mistake and pull off the highway. You can count more magpies
and horses than people, except for the teenagers who stand alongside
the dirt road, staring into the distance at something you can neither see
nor imagine.

It's the Sunday of a long weekend celebrating Christopher Columbus Day.
Somewhere else someone is working hard to *Make America Great Again.*

You stop at the rail crossing while the coal-filled cars roll by on the
groaning tracks.
On your right is the First Crow Indian Baptist Church, but you wait,
cross over to the IGA,
where the lot is filled with rusted-out pickup trucks.

Behind the counter, Terry, the kind-eyed Crow man, wearing a bone
and bead
choker, a dark brown eagle feather in the band of his white cowboy hat,
sets you straight as to your whereabouts:

"You can take the scenic route or backtrack to get to where you need to be.
Either way, you'll be just fine. You're in a hurry to get where you're
going, boy.
That's why you're lost."

On the highway again, the sign in your rear-view mirror reads:
Leaving Crow Country. Travel Well. Please Come Back.

PRUNING

for B, and for our fathers, W and E

This particular pile of rocks. In the backyard. In the middle of the Town of Pense. On the south Saskatchewan plains. Northern prairie. Or what used to be mixed-grass prairie, before it all fell under the plow, a phrase that makes you think of how a man, working alone, might climb down from a tractor, a Massey Ferguson, stumble and fall beneath the dual rear tires, and how the red machine unexpectedly rolls. How he lies there dying, staring up through tear-filled eyes at the July-blue afternoon sky. A few scattered clouds and, near the horizon, a murder of crows in flight and raising a racket at something the man cannot and will never see.

Will has no place when faced—faced down—by necessity.

These rocks from the south bank of the Red Deer, between Erwood and Hudson Bay, just downstream from where it bends and turns. Where the river changes not just its course, but also its mind, its pattern of thought, under counsel from the land. The elm forest there, and the four-foot-tall ferns in the deep leaf-shade. If you were a boy, if it was autumn and the water was low, there would be pools in which pike had become trapped and hungry. You could walk out on the stones, down the middle of the river, pretend you were performing a miracle—walking on water with the late-September sun warm on your face, skipping from pool to pool with your fibreglass rod and tackle box in hand, attach a five-of-diamonds to the leader and carefully toss the hook into those silty pools. At the end of the day, you might have five fish on a string to take home, to fry a meal for yourself and your silent, brooding father, just as distant then as now, more than a quarter century after you buried him.

But today, memory amounts to mythology.

This pile of rocks arrived in the bed of a half-ton truck, a Ford, driven 250 miles south by a childhood friend to whom you no longer speak because sometimes that's what men do, even after such an act of faith. The two of you unloaded them. And later, alone, you planted seeds, purple lupine that you have watched grow, bloom, and go to seed again, the only resurrection we can know. Even now, in mid-winter, the rocks breathe. You might think that's a metaphor or some disease of the mind, imagination perhaps, but the rocks breathe, my friend. You might not notice because their breathing is slow, a pace more patient than we can imagine.

Near the pile of rocks stand the apple trees. This autumn you finally had to admit one of them would no longer bear fruit. For a second straight year it was barren, and you had to accept it wasn't drought. When you got the chainsaw out of the shed and fired it up, the machine emitted a cloud of blue smoke, then a guttural roar like a pickup truck on its way south carrying a heavy load, shifting gears before accelerating hard, climbing the highway into the Porcupine Hills. You cut the three diverging trunks from the main. The centres were hollowed out at their cores. You understood why the tree was no longer bearing fruit.

You understood that *rotted-into-emptiness*
was true of your own heart, too.

So, there you stood, in the middle of the backyard on a Saturday afternoon, the chainsaw gripped and cooling in your left hand, wiping a bit of sweat from your brow with the back of your right, when the tears began to well in your eyes. And soon you were crying. Weeping. Openly. And you were embarrassed, even slightly ashamed, though there was no witness except the two dogs, one on either side, muzzles raised in concern, taking turns rubbing and then leaning their weights against your legs.

Yet you felt relieved, too, *unburdened* might be the word, like the branch of a tree in the spring after a night of heavy, wet snow, when the next day the clouds break, the sun comes out, a warm breeze arrives from the west, and the snow begins to melt, slips and falls to the ground, and the branch, though not yet returning to life, lifts ever so slightly, rises toward the sky, and, without being conscious of it, feels much lighter than it had, just a moment before.

LAND CLAIM

How many more times can you say the names of those rivers before
you begin to try the patience of the reader with each word and line of
yet another poem the need for which you both have begun to doubt?

On the north side, where the Fir empties into the Red Deer, there is
a sand point where you stand, while on the south side, the Etomami
comes flowing into the Red Deer, too. This is a memory. You've
been away thirty years now from your childhood home and hardly
visit anymore. Still, if you say it plain, it is the one place in the world
your heart shines like a rock lifted from the water before the sheen
begins to fade in the still-warm air and long September sunlight.

This is just remembrance. Nothing real lives on this page. And the
reader is unlikely to ever visit that place to see for themselves.

So, what's the point in going on about it?
Are you just making noise?

You wonder if this continual return is just about your own
mortality. Are you afraid? You know the rivers have carried on
doing what they do whether you were thinking about them
or not, whether you sat down to write something or not. You
know this. And you don't feel afraid. Not yet. Death is coming,
but you still have years ahead. Yet you keep looking back.

The land, it seems, is like that—it stakes a claim
and holds on dearly, no matter how far
we take ourselves away.

POEM FOR A FRIEND TRAVELLING

We are each a door or
a window, open wide—
everything enters, passes
through, and out the other
side, except like plastic
shopping bags caught in
the branches of trees
some things snag, catch,
take hold, and stay.

Memory's like that.

The occasional stubborn
thought, hanging on as if
it had claws. Those things
that stick grow into our
flesh, become part of us,
like tumours—
a father's dull silences,
a mother's bladed words.

But then there's the woman
on a beach across the Pacific
Ocean, in New Zealand, who
picks up a rock, holds it in her palm
and with her eyes. It has been brought
to her by the surge and slide of the
water. She will carry the grey-black
stone home with her, place it on
a windowsill in the sun beside
a flowering plant in a pot. Even
in moments when she forgets it,
the weight of its body remains
there in her hand.

You want to tell her right now,
in the moment before she first
picks it up, that you understand
her desire to in some way be
the glide of the swallow's wings
you watch this evening, high up
in the mid-summer air. To be
that sleek. That kind of free.

A BRIEF HISTORICAL ATLAS OF THE CANADIAN PRAIRIE, CONFIGURED AS AN ABANDONED RAIL YARD

Our lives are boundaried and bordered, defined and delimited,
on either side, the before and the after, by our proximity to
non-existence, before our births and after our deaths, an infinite
absence of this thing that is not a thing, that is substanceless
and without weight, but that we call a self, or some a soul.

Little more than a name.

For an *Indian*, the far side of either boundary is exactly what
governments dream for us, sometimes it seems the very reason
bureaucracy, a House of Parliament with its seats, came into
being. The wish we had never been, or once we are born,
the wish for us to die, to disappear. That simple, really.

Until there is not a single Indian left in Canada, acidic
on every lip, but no one will say *Genocide*.

Our lives are truly and always liminal spaces, neither the right
nor the wrong side of the tracks, but rather the rail yard itself,
with its gleaming strips of criss-crossed, oxidized steel tracks
and the lonely, upright switches waiting empty-handed and
empty-eyed, creosote-soaked timbers and crushed-rock beds,
the poisoned soil, the roar of engines and clank of cars, the
thunder of metal couplings, the stench of combusted diesel,
the severed limbs of men and the muffled cries of women, the
clink of bottles tipped and drained of alcohol, and later, the
sharp-edged glint of shattered glass, the lichen-encrusted
loading docks and the padlocked doors with their pig-iron
tint, guarding the dust-choked emptiness inside warehouses
where darkness is stored. And the silence left when it all stops.

The sudden, silent radiance of everything that
is useless, abandoned, and forgotten.

In that quiet, stirred by the slightest breeze, is the flowering
jimson weed, its creamy trumpet-shaped blooms opening at night,
inviting the sphinx moths to come, to feed in the moonlight.

ECDYSIS

Mid-afternoon, in the passenger seat of a rusting Ford F-150, you spotted a bald eagle perched in a dead cottonwood alongside the grid road, and dust rose up all around when your friend slammed on the brakes. It's true, there is no other word for it, the bird was *magnificent*—twenty feet up, gripping the branch with its scaled feet and two-inch talons and looking directly at you before lifting off and, with a few beats of its wings, drifting lazily away like slow smoke over the stubble fields in the just-now-gathering dusk.

Sunday, and god was nowhere to be found, again.

But that's okay. You have sat with your losses. In the dirt hills throughout the drought. And no deity spoke to you. There are no words. But the sagebrush, the cacti, and the rattlesnake passing you by without notice taught you to sit quietly as sun and moon and stars and another thick-bodied cloud carried on with *being*. Each came and went and left no trace.

Except for the snake that left its opaque skin in a hollow at the top of the sand ridge. What it left behind was empty, a kind of hole, an absence, a fragility that you could pick up and hold in your hand. And that's enough. That was just what you always needed to know.

THE RITUAL IS DANGEROUS

It is alive, has a beak with teeth,
like a raven with the head
of a molosser-type dog.
It has claws.

The simplest advice is this:
be careful who you ask to dinner;
the spirit you invite is never
the one who arrives.

THE WEIGHT

Red-breasted nuthatch
in the apple tree, beak
buried deep in the frozen flesh
seeking seeds, and thirteen
Canada geese flying overhead
in the expected V. Nothing here
to see or remark upon. Just

February in Saskatchewan,
snow falling, a breakfast
of boiled eggs with a cup
of green tea, a bit of reading,
and silence descending,
again, like the heavy pull
of age and gravity.

LITTLE PRAYER

after Danez Smith & for K.

let ruin end here
and rapture, too, since

in this world rapture is just
another kind of desolation

let the woman find honey
where honey always was

in the deep hollow of a birch tree
where sweetness looked like slaughter

let her enter the black bear's den
to find aurora sightless, but dreaming stars

dreaming the birth of a creature such as she
into the light and the lilies of the field

finding in this life something sweet
if only occasionally and far between

let this be
a healing and a wounding,

a wounding and a healing,
again

SONG OF AUTUMN

Those who know do not speak;
those who speak will never know.

Beware of this: language discriminates—
this thing is not that thing. But *it is,* even if

metaphor fails to build its bridge.
Better to listen to the birds and trees,

walk in the rain, in the low valley
by the creek with its broken

cottonwoods, red-winged blackbirds,
and wind in the reeds. The bulrush's

song of autumn. Patience. A bit of solitude.
If you are lucky, the land will unmask you.

13 LINES FOR CHARLES WRIGHT

You stand in the backyard dark and answer to the night
for *this thing* you have been and *that one* you have not,
for all the friends who have come and gone, or who never
arrived at your door, or did, only to find it closed and locked.

The Perseid meteors stroke the sky with streaks of light, the grass
gone dormant beneath your feet, sheathed in the bright-beaded
deerskin moccasins someone, decades ago, gifted you

—and what the past has to say is silence, pretty much that,
        and nothing else—

thick-bodied moths bob among the branches of the cherry tree,
last leaves rustled by a September breeze, and a quartet of bats
weaves sinuous paths in the absence of moonlight.

And you know, your soul, your spirit has nothing to do with
        heaven or eternity.
Just these things, here and now, that you can touch and see.

ODE FOR SPRING

I.

March. The blackbirds have arrived, have returned.
Their voices are a polyphony of flute notes, lifted
on the warm west wind this afternoon. It is spring,
and I, too, am filled with release. Overflowing.
I wonder if you hear my voice, old ones,
my grandmothers and grandfathers.
I am singing.

I want you to know I have not forgotten.
Everything is close, is near. Nothing
has been forgotten. Afternoon song
leads into night song and carries on
into the next morning.
Through the night
the starlight is old, older even than
the stones. And nothing is lost.

II.

All the things I do not know, all the names
I do not know, I carry with me, still,
inside my bones.

READING A POETRY MANUSCRIPT ON A SATURDAY MORNING: A WARNING

The greatest danger you face is getting lost in the words, in the pursuit
 of a single idea,
forgetting, just outside your back door, the late-August ripening
 of plums and cherries.

In the grey light and rain, green leaves soon to be gone—

the lone sparrow there.

CEREMONY TO SUMMON DREAMS

The woman stands at the kitchen window above the sink,
eating a soft-poached egg on a piece of lightly toasted rye,

watching through the thin glass pane
the juncos gathered at the feeder.

This is the first day of their return,
and, taken in by that illusion of a self
shed like the last phase of the moon,
this is what she calls joy.

And who will say she is wrong?
Who can say such a reverie is not real,
just because it is passing rapidly away
like every other moment
in this world?

After her meal, the hours bring all the small
concerns that make up a day—

crosswords marched across a page, and faces, but only
in memory (as the minutes come and go in solitude),
dishes to be washed, elderly parents to be phoned,
and an impatient shepherd dog to be walked
around the block and along the path by
the still, black waters of the lake.

At bedtime, she will swathe her slight body
in soft brushed cotton and slip between
the white sheets, beneath the duvet.

And despite each task having been completed with care,
the familiar fear is with her—
what have I done this day to earn my keep?

Anxiety a small emptiness in her heart
just the size of the mottled stone
on the nightstand
by the bed. She tumbles
toward restless sleep.

At midnight, the wind runs
like the body of a horse
through the pliable branches
of spruce and pine.

A heavy rain falls into
the sharp-spined needles.
Only a few droplets find
the dark backs and breathing
breasts of the sheltering birds.

Beneath the shattered, lightning-split sky

—tongued grasses, bright-faced flowers,
the exploding roots of trees—

the green fuse of the force that drives
everything   is lit.

PELICANS

What you want is not Orpheus singing songs so the trees
pull up their roots and follow the words and the music of the
lyre: that terrible beauty and power, a too-human violence.

No wonder his sisters tore him apart.

What you want is the woman listening to the singing corn
leaves, the stalks as they bend in the breeze. Walking the field
edge, she need not die to become the green shoots of spring.

What happens happens forever yet never happens enough.
Like the three enormous pelicans lifting awkwardly off the
thin, crooked finger of the lake at the bottom of the valley, each
body a blaze of white in the mid-afternoon sun. Their black-
tipped wings bear a wisdom beyond what you can say, and
you want to watch this unfolding for the rest of your days.

Wouldn't that be something, my friend? Wouldn't it be enough?

TÂPWÊ

Nothing above, nothing below.

The stars, untold light years away,
the earth beneath your feet, all of this

dwells inside your heart; your heart
dwells there, too, inside the near and far.

No near and far. No room for belief.
No room for fear.

Just what is and is and is.

*tâpwê—it's true, truth

ACKNOWLEDGEMENTS

Gratitude to friends and family whose care, compassion, and love has endured the knowledge of what I have been. I don't need to name you; you know who you are. If you are unsure if you are included, count yourself in.

Many thanks to editor Laurie D. Graham for her patience and perseverance with this project and The Mucker who spent too much time mucking around with his words.

Thank you to Frog Hollow Press, founder Caryl Peters, and editor Shane Neilson for the chapbook *In the Dark Times,* in which some of these poems first appeared.

Thanks to the magazines, and their editors, in which others of these poems first appeared.

I would be remiss not to offer a big thank you to the staff at URP for all the work they do, especially on the Oskana Series, and to Copy Editor Kelly Laycock for setting me straight more than once.

Finally, Alex and Mabel, Rita and Gracie—each of you a gift I did not earn and could not deserve. Canine companions who did their best to teach me that I could be better than what I was. Truly the best kind of people.

Award-winning poet Randy Lundy is a Cree, Irish, and Norwegian member of the Barren Lands First Nation, Brochet, Manitoba. Born in Thompson, Manitoba, he lived most of his life in Saskatchewan before recently taking a teaching position at University of Toronto Scarborough.

He is the author of four full-length books of poetry, *Field Notes for the Self* (2020) and *Blackbird Song* (2018) with University of Regina Press, *Gift of the Hawk* (2005) and *Under the Night Sun* (1999) with Coteau Books, as well as the chapbook *In the Dark Times* (2022) with Frog Hollow Press.

ᐅᐢᑲᓇ

OSKANA POETRY & POETICS

BOOK SERIES

Publishing new and established authors, Oskana Poetry
& Poetics offers both contemporary poetry at its best
and probing discussions of poetry's cultural role.

Randy Lundy—*Series Editor*

PREVIOUS BOOKS IN THE SERIES:

Dog and Moon, by Kelly Shepherd (2025)

The Salmon Shanties: A Cascadian Song Cycle, by Harold Rhenisch (2024)

Into the Continent, by Emily McGiffin (2024)

Wrack Line, by M.W. Jaeggle (2023)

Dislocations, by Karen Enns (2023)

The History Forest, by Michael Trussler (2022)

Synaptic, by Alison Calder (2022)

Shifting Baseline Syndrome, by Aaron Kreuter (2022)

Pitchblende, by Elise Marcella Godfrey (2021)

Red Obsidian, by Stephan Torre (2021)

Burden, by Douglas Burnet Smith (2020)

Field Notes for the Self, by Randy Lundy (2020)

Live Ones, by Sadie McCarney (2019)

Forty-One Pages: On Poetry, Language, and Wilderness, by John Steffler (2019)

Blackbird Song, by Randy Lundy (2018)

The House of Charlemagne, by Tim Lilburn (2018)

Cloud Physics, by Karen Enns (2017)

The Long Walk, by Jan Zwicky (2016)

Measures of Astonishment: Poets on Poetry,
presented by the League of Canadian Poets (2016)

Praise for *No Middle Path: The Civil War in Kerry*

'Owen O'Shea brings a mature realism to the documenting of revolutionary Kerry a century ago, underpinned by original, comprehensive archival research that allows him to confront difficult questions and let the compelling personal testimonies of the combatants and their families breathe.'

Professor Diarmaid Ferriter, Professor of Modern Irish History, UCD

'Nowhere was the hatred greater, the conflict more brutal, than in Kerry, as is detailed in this superb study, which offers an even-handed, detailed and well-written account of the war and its aftermath in the county.'

Dr David McCullagh, historian and author

'One of the best [books] the Decade of Centenaries has produced.'

Donal Fallon, historian and author

Praise for *Ballymacandy: The Story of a Kerry Ambush*

'Colourful details help to lift Owen O'Shea's reconstruction of the Ballymacandy gunfight well above your average local history ... O'Shea does a fine job of uncovering the story's lesser-known tangents ... Meticulously researched and soberly written.'

Andrew Lynch, *Sunday Business Post*

'This is local history at its best: clearly written and cliché free, painstakingly researched, a useful index, a really clear map, interesting photos and placing the ambush in the context of Irish history at the time and its aftermath.'

John Kirkaldy, *Books Ireland*

Owen O'Shea, a native of Milltown, County Kerry, is a historian and the author of several books on history and politics in his native county, including the highly acclaimed *No Middle Path: The Civil War in Kerry* (Merrion Press, 2022). Other books include *Ballymacandy: The Story of a Kerry Ambush* (Merrion Press, 2021) and *Heirs to the Kingdom: Kerry's Political Dynasties* (O'Brien Press, 2011). He was co-author, with Gordon Revington, of *A Century of Politics in the Kingdom: A County Kerry Compendium* (Merrion Press, 2018). He was also co-editor of a history of Kerry and the Easter Rising in 2016 with Bridget McAuliffe and Mary McAuliffe, with whom he jointly organised and hosted the Kerry Civil War Conference in 2023. He works as Media, Communications and Customer Relations Officer with Kerry County Council and holds a PhD from the School of History at University College Dublin. For more about Owen, see www.owenoshea.ie.